BIRTHDAY BOY

Thomas Ogren

Bedford County Literacy Council
Chestnut Ridge Senior High School
2588 Quaker Valley Road
New Paris, PA 15554-8612

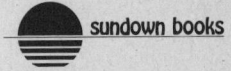
sundown books

New Readers Press • Syracuse, New York

This novel is a work of fiction. Names, characters, places, and incidents either are the products of the author's imagination or are used fictitiously, and any resemblance to actual persons, living or dead, events, or locales is entirely coincidental.

The publisher wishes to thank Ray Rinaldi and the North Area Boys Club of Syracuse, New York, for their help in creating the photograph on the front cover.

ISBN 0-88336-211-2

©1988, 1990
New Readers Press
Publishing Division of Laubach Literacy International
Box 131, Syracuse, New York 13210

All rights reserved. No part of this book may be reproduced or transmitted in any form or by any means, electronic or mechanical, including photocopying, recording, or by any information storage and retrieval system, without permission in writing from the publisher.

Printed in the United States of America

Edited by Kay Koschnick
Illustrations by Kevin D. Aldrich
Cover design by Chris Steenwerth
Cover photo by Hal Silverman Studio

9 8 7 6 5 4 3 2 1

To Yvonne,
a wonderful wife,
who has stuck with me
for better or worse,
in good times and bad.

Prologue

There's a little cafe in St. Paul, Minnesota, called The Birthday Boy's Place. And although it isn't much of a restaurant, the food is good. The pies at The Birthday Boy's Place are the best in town. The story of the cafe itself is something.

Chapter 1

She wrapped the little black baby in a warm blanket and walked down the empty street. It was late at night, very dark but warm for the month of May. She walked down the street as fast as she could. At the corner of Jackson and 14th Streets, she left the baby boy on a bus stop bench. She knew that it was wrong. It just had to be. But no one was ever going to find out that this baby had been hers.

A St. Paul policeman, Tom Oaks, found the little baby. He took him to the nearest hospital. The doctors at the hospital found the baby to be healthy.

The nurses thought he needed a name. They agreed that since he had been found on Jackson Street, he would be called Jackson. The policeman who found him was Tom Oaks, so they decided to call the new baby boy Jackson Oaks.

The nurses didn't know exactly when he had been born. It was now May, so for a birth date, they just filled in May and the year.

Jackson Oaks was sent to a small Catholic orphanage in St. Paul. He spent the first three years of his life in the orphanage. He was then placed with an Italian family who had four other foster children. After seven months, the family asked the orphanage to take him back. He cried all the time, they said. And he wet the bed. And he didn't talk at all.

The orphanage was his home for another year. At the age of four, Jackson was adopted by a Portuguese family who had five children of their own and three other adopted ones. His adopted parents were Sam and Sonia Fernandez. They were strict, hardworking parents who tried their best not to play favorites. Jackson was sent to a nearby Catholic school with his new brothers and sisters. At school, he was good at sports, but lousy at math and reading.

The Fernandezes tried to get him to study harder in school. They tried to see that he always did his homework. Mostly, though, they failed.

The boy found it hard to sit still in class. His teachers said that he was "hyperactive." Often, Jackson was kicked out of school for fighting with other boys. Each time, Sam Fernandez asked him who had started the fight and who had won. He was told in each case that Jackson had not started the fight. And Jackie always seemed to win.

Sam said that he was glad that his son wasn't a bully. He was also glad that the boy won the fights. "Don't ever start no fights," said Sam Fernandez. "But if you get pushed too far, start fighting. And remember, when you're fighting, it's a lot better to win than to lose."

This talk with his adopted father had a deep and lasting effect on Jackson. Years later, he sometimes thought it was just about the only talk he could remember having with Sam. Except for their talks about his birthday, of course.

He had noticed early on that all the other children—in his family, at school, at the orphanage, even—had birthdays. Everyone had a birthday, everyone except him. He complained about this to his adopted parents. Why, he asked, was it that everyone except him had a birthday?

"Because you just ain't got one, is why," said Sam.

"But it ain't fair!" said Jackson.

"*Isn't* fair," said Sonia.

"Isn't, ain't, whatever!" Jackson cried. "Everyone else has one."

"I suppose that's true," said Sam. "It isn't fair, really. Kids like having birthdays. But you'll see, Jackie. When you get older, you'll be happy not having a birthday. When you get on in years, birthdays just kind of remind you how old you're getting and how much money you never made."

These answers were never quite enough for the boy. Often, he daydreamed that his real parents would suddenly show up. They would have a really good reason for leaving him on that bus stop bench. They would be nice people. Of course, they would be happy that they had finally found him. And then, too, they would know the exact day that he was born. He would have a birthday.

Jackson often brought up the subject of his not having a birthday. Sam and Sonia would talk about it together. They would agree that there really should be some day set aside for his birthday.

Somehow, though, what with trying to raise so many kids and everything else, they never quite got around to it.

Chapter 2

In the eighth grade, Jackson was held back a year. He was having lots of trouble with math and English. Halfway through his second year of the eighth grade, he started cutting classes. Each time he would get caught and get a lecture from Sam and Sonia. This happened five times in less than a month.

At last, Sam took the boy aside and told him: "Now you listen to me, Jackie. If you're going to go to school, you're going to go. There can't be no halfway about it. If you don't go to school, then you're going to have to work."

"OK," said Jackie quickly. "I'd rather work. Like you do, Dad."

"Work ain't all fun," said Sam. "Sometimes it's pretty lousy."

"So is school," said Jackie. "For me, anyhow."

"OK," said Sam. "I'll see what I can find for you."

What he found was a job that almost nobody else wanted. Near their house was a turkey plant. Every day, big trucks brought thousands of live turkeys there. Every day, these turkeys were slaughtered, plucked, cleaned, wrapped, and sent out to stores. Jackson got the job of cleaning up after the gutting crew.

The turkeys came hanging upside down, feathered and flopping down the line. One man would kill them, slicing their throats with a razor-sharp knife. The big birds would then go into a vat of scalding water. From there, they went into the machine that plucked off their feathers. Next, the birds came down the line, and women cut them open. Certain parts, like the liver and gizzard, were saved. The guts, or offal, as it was called, were dumped into the large sinks.

Jackson ran around scooping up the offal into a large bushel pail with a handle on each side. When the pail was full, he took it outside and threw the turkey guts into a dump truck. Each day, the dump truck would be empty when he started and full when he left.

"A few days at this job and the boy will be happy to go back to school," Sam told Sonia.

Sam was wrong, though. Jackson got a special work pass from the school. He was now 14. He was to learn the turkey business and study schoolwork at home. What he learned about was turkey offal.

The work at the plant was never-ending. It would have been hard for a grown man. The place was filthy and smelled bad, but Jackson worked right along. Everyone in the turkey plant yelled at him. It was always, "Do this!" "Hurry up, kid!" But Jackson didn't mind. He was working like Sam did. He was earning his own money. Pretty soon, he wouldn't need other people to support him.

The grownups could yell at him all they wanted. He wasn't going to let it bother him. As long as he kept up with the work, they wouldn't fire him. And keep up he did.

Jackson gave half of his paycheck to his parents and was allowed to keep the other half for himself. Every week, the boss at the plant gave him a dressed turkey to take home. At first, he hated to eat turkey after working around it all day. But after a while, this no longer bothered him. He almost even grew to like it.

Jackson also grew to like having his own money. For a boy so young, he was careful with his cash. Each paycheck, he would put 10 dollars in the bank. The rest he would spend.

Jackie always made sure that he had a good present for each of his brothers and sisters on their birthdays. Sometimes one of them would say it sure was crummy that Jackie didn't have a birthday. He would just shrug and say that it didn't matter to him. It did, though. It bothered him terribly. After every birthday in the family, he would go upstairs and lie on his bed and cry secretly into his pillow.

Chapter 3

The years passed quickly. Jackie's brothers and sisters went to school and brought home good report cards. Jackson went to work and brought home his paycheck. After a while, the grownups at the plant stopped yelling at him so much. He wasn't a bad kid, really, they said. He didn't talk much, it was true. But, man, he could sure handle turkey guts!

Every year, the boss took Jackson aside and told him that he was doing a good job. Each year, he got a small raise in pay. The work no longer seemed so hard to him. He grew quickly, sprouting several inches each year. His legs became thin and hard from running around the plant. The muscles in his arms and shoulders thickened. His chest became solid and deep. By the age of 16, he had a build that anyone would admire.

When Jackson was 17, something happened that changed the rest of his life.

He was walking home from work at the turkey plant. As he rounded a corner, he saw three guys, older than he, standing talking to a couple of girls.

One of the girls was tall and very nice-looking. Jackson looked at her as he walked by. He didn't wink his eye, nod his head, or anything of the sort. He just looked. He was no more than 10 feet past them when one of the guys yelled at him. "Hey, you!" he yelled. "You, boy!"

"You talking to me?" asked Jackson as he turned around.

"That's right," said the tallest of the three. "Come on over here, nigger."

Jackson Oaks Fernandez, turkey guts hauler, stood where he had turned. He hadn't been in a fight since he'd quit the eighth grade. He looked at the guy who called him a nigger. The guy was probably at least 20 years old. So were his two friends.

Maybe they're drunk, Jackson thought. Probably just trying to have some fun at my expense. But still, Jackson stayed put where he was. The three of them were all larger and heavier than he was. Football players from the University of Minnesota, most likely.

"You got big eyes," said the tall one. "Buggy nigger eyes, if you ask me. Why don't you keep them to yourself, boy?"

Jackson said nothing. He remembered what Sam had told him. "Don't ever start no fights. But if you get pushed too far, start fighting. And remember, it's a lot better to win than to lose."

So Jackson just stood there, saying nothing. He'd never been all that quick with the words, anyway. Talking had never done much except get him in trouble. He sized up the three young men. All of them seemed to think it was pretty darn funny. Jackson didn't think it was funny, though. Not in the least.

The two girls were also looking at him. They weren't laughing, though, just looking.

"Did you hear me, boy?" said the loud one again. "You ain't saying much, are you?"

Jackson said nothing.

"I guess you're just yellow. Yeah, that's it. You're a bug-eyed, yellow nigger!"

Jackson stared at him, cold anger building up slowly in his chest. The guy was wrong, calling him chicken. He wasn't afraid. Not now. Not about fighting. Standing up in the classroom, having to answer the teacher's questions—that used to frighten him. Using big words in a conversation bothered him. Never knowing if he would say or use the words in the right way—that scared him. But this guy didn't intimidate him. Loudmouths like this guy would never scare him. He'd been yelled at by better.

The big guy turned to his friends. "Come on, guys. Let's teach this nigger boy some manners." They walked toward him slowly, laughing.

When they were almost within arm's reach, Jackson lunged at them. He swung wildly with his right fist and took the biggest one square on the chin. The other two rushed at him. He put his head down and threw punches blindly from all angles. From his crouch, he lashed out at them. He felt his fists sinking into soft bellies, crashing against hard heads.

Jackson swung twice more, hitting only the air, when he noticed that all three of them were on the ground. The loudmouth looked to be out cold. One of the others was sitting on the sidewalk, holding his nose. The other one lay on his side, moaning.

Jackson looked at the two girls. They looked almost as surprised as he felt. He turned around and started walking away from the scene.

"Hey! Hey, man, stop!" he heard someone yell.

He quickened his step, resisting the urge to start running. Maybe it was the police. "Hey, man, stop, will you?" he heard from behind him.

Turning around, he saw a short, balding little man in a rumpled gray suit, running after him.

Jackson stopped. The man certainly didn't look like the police. "Whew!" said the man, trying to catch his breath. "I thought I was going to lose you. My name's Frankie Carbella." He stuck out his hand for Jackson to shake. "What's your name, son?"

"Jackson Oaks Fernandez."

"Jackson Oaks, huh?" said the little man, pumping Jackson's hand. He was surprisingly strong for such a small fellow. "Oaks. I like that. Strong as an oak tree. Let's go get a sandwich or something, Mr. Fernandez. I think you're just the fighter I've been looking for. For a long time, too."

And thus was Jackson Oaks Fernandez's boxing career started.

Chapter 4

They weighed Jackson on a scale at the gym. "One hundred and fifty-seven pounds," said Frankie Carbella. "You're a middleweight."

For his first fight, they had Jackie lie about his age. He was supposed to be 18, and no one doubted him when he said that he was.

For his first opponent, they matched him with a fat welterweight who smoked too much and trained too little. For two rounds, the overweight fighter jabbed him, slapped him all around the ring, and cut him deeply over the left eye. Then he ran out of gas.

Jackson hit him solidly three times in the third round. He knocked him out at the start of the fourth.

His trainer and now manager, Frankie, took him to the hospital to have his eyebrow stitched. "You done real good, Jackson," he told him. "You got a head like a rock, man. Like a rock! And you can punch, too. Boy, can you punch!"

The manager left him in the waiting room. After almost an hour, a nurse—tall, black, and businesslike—led him into the emergency room. She started to clean his wound.

"How did you get this?" she asked.

"Fighting," bragged Jackson. "In the ring, you know. I'm a boxer. A pro."

"A pro, are you? You don't look old enough to me."

"I'm eighteen," lied Jackson, thinking that it was funny how easy it was to lie, once you got the hang of it. "Yep," he said, "I'm a professional fighter. My manager says I'm going to make a lot of money."

"I suppose that's what they tell you," said the nurse.

Jackson felt her strong hands cleaning his forehead. He tried to look at her as she worked on him. She was a nice lady. Kind of cute, too, in a bossy sort of way. She was probably real smart. He could tell.

"Hold still," she ordered him. "And so, Mr. Pro, what happened in the fight? Did you win?"

"You bet I did!" beamed Jackson. "I knocked him out in the fourth round. It was my first match."

"Oh, I see," she said. "Were you afraid?"

"Yeah, sure I was. Afraid I'd make a fool of myself in front of all those people."

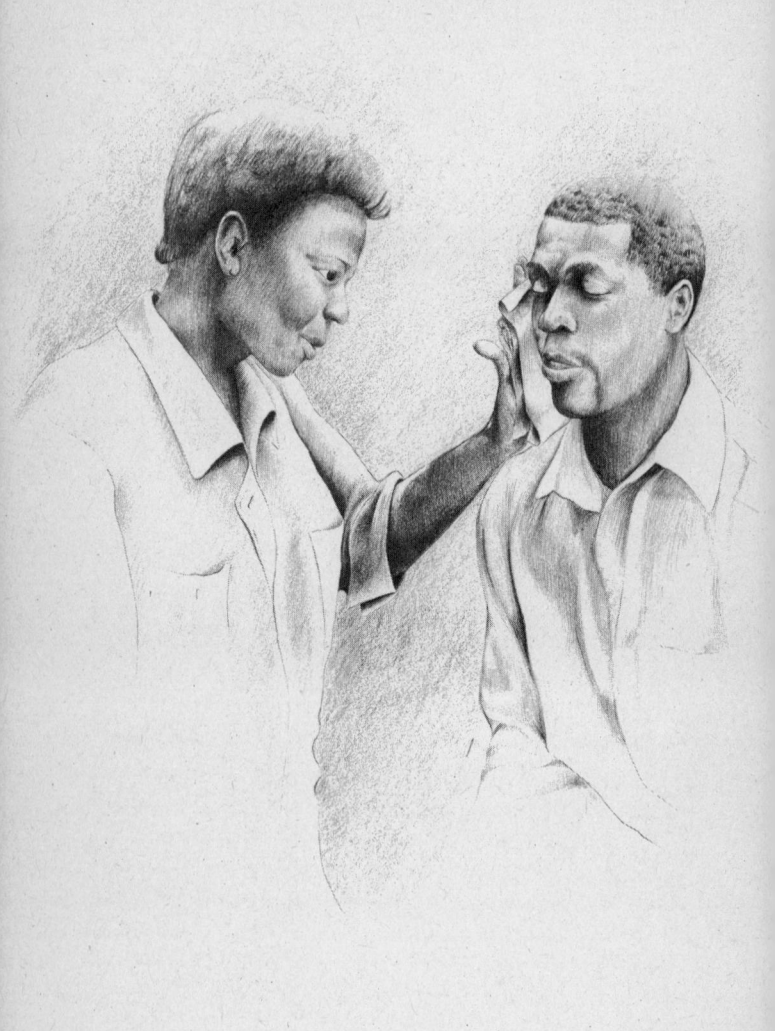

"But you weren't afraid of the other fighter?"

"Him? No, I wasn't afraid of him. Shoot, I wasn't even thinking about him."

"Is that right? Was he white or black?"

"Who?"

"The other fighter. The one that put this gash in your eyebrow."

Jackson laughed. "What difference does it make? It didn't matter to me. He was fat, though. He was hitting me pretty good, too, till he got tired. Say," and he paused, for he had never before asked the question he now wanted to ask. "Say," he repeated himself. "My name's Jackie Fernandez. What's your name?"

"My name?" she asked back. "What do you care?"

"Well," he said, "I'd just like to know. What is it, a secret or something?"

"No," she said and laughed. "I guess not. My name is Madeline Davis."

"Madeline," he said. "That's a nice name. Maybe—" And he stopped. He was trying to get out exactly the right words. It wasn't easy. Suddenly, his stomach felt tight. His whole body seemed to go cold, as though it knew he was about to make a fool out of himself yet.

"Maybe what?" asked Madeline.

"Well," said Jackson. "Maybe we could go out sometime. You know, to a movie or something."

"Yeah?" she said. "Who knows? Stranger things have happened." And for a second, she said nothing. "Well," she said at last, "I've got to go. The doctor will be in to sew you up in just a minute. And, Jackie, next time keep your hands up."

"Right," he said. "I'm going to do that. I'm going to start training and everything. You'll see."

"OK," she said, and as she left the room, she smiled at him.

She's got a mighty fine smile, he thought. Mighty fine.

The doctor sewed him up and discharged him. In the dark of the late night, Jackie walked slowly home. It had been some evening. In his pocket was his pay—a crisp $100 bill. And neatest of all was the nurse, Madeline. She hadn't laughed at him when he had sort of asked her out. She said maybe. And *maybe* was a whole lot better than *no*.

Chapter 5

Jackson started training in a big way. The boss at the turkey plant now let him off work an hour and a half early each day. He ran to the gym and started learning the trade. An old ex-pug, with one bluish dead eye, taught him how to use his left hand. The left, he learned, was really more important than the right. Anybody could throw a right, they said. Not everyone knew how to use the left.

If he wanted to make the big money, he was told, he needed lots of knockouts. The fans liked to see knockouts. Frankie Carbella came around now and then and told him he was looking good.

Carbella arranged for Jackson's next fight. He told the promoter that Jackson had the makings of a main-eventer. "The kid is perfect," he said. "He's going to be a dandy middleweight. Weighs one-fifty-seven. And he's tall. About six feet, I think. He's got them

25

skinny legs, you know. And shoulders and arms like a heavyweight.

"The kid's good, I tell you. For one thing, he can't box at all. The fans like to see a guy that ain't afraid to get hit. He takes a punch real good, too. And he can punch. Hits like a sledgehammer."

In his second professional fight, Jackson was matched with a kid from Duluth called the Duluth Dynamo. The Dynamo had had only three professional fights himself. He had won all three of them by knockout. In the first round, he kept hitting Jackie with his jab. In the second round, he blackened both of Jackie's eyes. In the third round, Jackson started throwing the left hook short and tight the way he'd been instructed. He caught the Duluth kid coming in. He staggered him with the left and then clubbed him senseless with his right.

The crowd roared its approval. Coins were thrown into the ring. Jackson walked back to his corner. The referee took his arm and raised it high. The crowd erupted again. Jackson stared at the floor. His head throbbed from the solid punches he had taken. "Wave!" shouted his cornermen. "Wave to the people. They're nuts about you!"

Jackson looked out at the yelling fans. Their faces seemed to blur together. He waved his gloved fists, and the blur called out his name. They clapped and whistled. They smiled. As he walked back to the dressing room, people slapped him on the back. "Way to go!" they told him. "Good fight, man!"

Later, Frankie took him again to the hospital to have his lip repaired. Before he left, Frankie pressed three $50 bills into Jackson's hand. "There's going to be more coming," he told him. "Lots more. The purses are going to keep growing."

Chapter 6

The purses did keep growing. But best of all, in Jackson's mind, was his new and growing relationship with Madeline Davis. He had tried to ask her out at the hospital after his second fight. As he stumbled over the words, she stepped in and helped him out. "Sure, I'll go out with you," she said. "Why not?"

They made some pair, she thought. She was a 24-year-old nurse, black, poor but educated. Jackson could hardly read or write. He was, she thought, a soft-spoken, hard-hitting motherless kid.

Madeline had been a worker all of her life. She had grown up with three sisters. All of them were better looking than she was. All of them were more popular with the guys. But she had been the best student in the bunch. It was always Madeline who stayed up late doing extra book reports. Madeline was the one who had brought home the report cards stacked with *A*s.

She was now in her third year as a registered nurse. Most guys thought she was too tall, too big of foot, or too broad of shoulder. Most of the men she met didn't really think she was sexy or feminine. But now she had herself a man who thought she was perfect.

Sure, it was true that he was too young for her. And, yes, it was a fact that he could hardly read or write. He was just terrible at arithmetic. He could hardly carry on a conversation with a group of any size. It was all true. But still, he had promise—so much of it, it seemed. And, with her, he talked freely. He overflowed with things that before he had only thought about.

And Jackson cared about her. He needed her. Maybe she was just kind of a mother substitute for him. She didn't know. She didn't really care. She knew one thing for sure, though. She liked this quiet, tough kid. And he liked her. Maybe it was love.

Chapter 7

Jackson kept training. He learned how to throw short punches and fight inside. He learned to throw his punches in threes. First the jab, then the right cross, followed by the left hook.

The trainers showed him how to spin the other fighters off the ropes. They taught him how to pull their hands down with a left and then punch with the right.

He learned how to hit the heavy bag. The heavy bag was tough. If you hit the heavy bag at all wrong, it hurt your wrist. But if you hit it right, it felt good. The heavy bag popped when you busted it just right.

Three weeks after his fight with the Dynamo, Jackson stepped into the ring with Macho Sanchez from Texas. Jackie got lucky and nailed him early in the first round.

Two weeks later, he was matched with Angel Estevos from Miami. Jackie dropped Estevos twice in the first round. He put him down for the 10 count in the second.

Later, Madeline said that Jackson must be getting better. He had now fought two fights in a row without needing any stitches.

A month after the Estevos fight, he was matched with Charlie Kish of Detroit. Kish had a record of six wins and two losses. Five of his wins had been by knockout. They said he was a dirty fighter.

In the first round, Kish hit Jackie with an overhand right and floored him. In the second round, the guy butted Jackson in a clinch, chipping one of Jackie's front teeth. In the third round, the man from Detroit smashed home a hard one-two. Jackson felt his nose give way. It was a bad, disgusting feeling. He would have this exact same feeling often in the coming years.

In the fourth round, Jackie started finding the range with a left hook to Kish's body. In the fifth round, they went at it toe-to-toe. They lashed out punishment on each other until Jackie landed his bomb. The Detroit man staggered. Jackson drilled him with a left. He slammed him with his right and knocked him cold with the left hook.

That night, Jackson sat on the couch at Madeline's apartment and held an ice bag to his nose. The nose had been put straight as best as could be done. It would never be the same again.

"Maybe," said Madeline, "you ought to find another way to earn money. I can't stand to see you get hurt like this."

Jackson tried to laugh. His mouth was sore, and the effort only made his nose feel bigger and more sensitive. "I beat him, didn't I?"

"Sure, you beat him. So what? Does that make your nose feel any better?"

"Uh-huh," he replied. "I think it does." Then, too, he had made $300 tonight. Three hundred dollars cash money. Now that was something! Even Madeline didn't make that kind of dough. And there would be more money coming, too. Frankie had promised. More money. Lots and lots of the green stuff.

It took several months for his nose to mend properly. During this time, he trained hard. Every morning before work, he ran seven miles. In the gym, he learned new tricks of the so-called sweet science. Old pros, long since punched out and retired, taught him how to hook after the jab. They showed him how to slip, duck, block, and parry punches. He learned how to roll with the force when he got clobbered. He learned how to feint and how not to telegraph his punches. Jackson absorbed it all. He argued with none of it. He worked harder than ever.

"Keep your hands up, baby!" Madeline told him as he went off to fight his sixth pro battle.

In the fight, he began to feel as though now at last he actually was a real boxer. The months of running and sparring were starting to pay off.

His opponent, Gorilla Mazon, was strong but slow. For the first three rounds, Jackson danced around the ring. He slapped Mazon with raking hooks. He riddled him with stiff jabs, parried punches, and evaded all the hard shots. At the close of the third round, Frankie Carbella jumped into his corner and screamed at him, "What the hell's the matter with you? You forget how to punch?"

"I am punching," said Jackson. "I'm beating him, ain't I?"

"I don't give a damn if you are or not!" yelled Frankie. "The fans here want to see you slug, man. They come to see a slugger, not some sissy, fancy stuff. Punch the guy out, will you? Come on!"

And suddenly it was the start of the fourth round. Gorilla Mazon rushed him. Jackson speared him with a jab and moved away. God, it was such a shame. Such a damn, rotten, stinking pity! For once, he was starting to feel

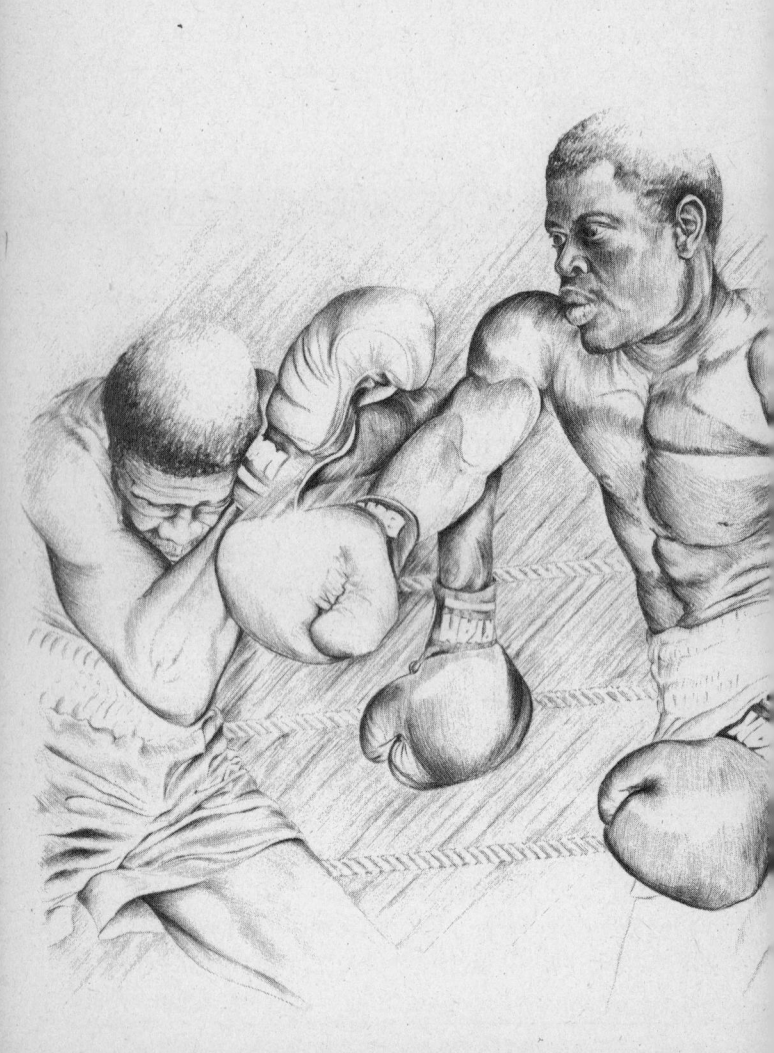

like a fine boxer instead of a pug. Like a graceful athlete instead of a crude animal. This Gorilla Whoever wasn't much of a fighter. It was almost a shame beating on him.

"Nail him!" he heard being screamed from his corner. "Nail him! Cream the guy! Kill him!"

And the next time Mazon rushed in, Jackie socked him with the short left hook. He jolted Mazon twice with uppercuts and then slammed him with powerful rights to the face. The Gorilla went down in a heap.

The crowd screamed and stomped their feet. They loved it! But Jackson felt cheapened. This was no sport; it was a business. A smashing, hitting, hurting business.

For his work that night, he was paid $450. He was also promised a bout on the next week's card. At Madeline's that night, they talked about it. "Quit," she told him again. But there was no way that he could. The money was too good. The claps on the back felt too nice. Then, too, there wasn't much of anything else that he did as well, except hauling turkey guts. And he had had about enough of that.

In his seventh match, he knocked out Cooper Larson in the second round. In his eighth fight, he stopped Animal Adams in the third. People were starting to take notice of him. In the gym one day, two young kids actually asked for his autograph. In his ninth fight, he polished off Freddie Rouse within 60 seconds of the opening round. "You're going places!" people told him. "You're going to be the champ!"

For fun—and just to see if he could—Jackie started cooking meals for Madeline and himself. Whenever he couldn't understand some of the words in the cookbook, Madeline helped him out. Each night, he fixed something different. Some of the meals he fixed were great. Some of them they fed to the dog next door.

Jackson Oaks Fernandez earned $1,000 for his 10th fight. It was his first 10-rounder. His first main event. His opponent, Chalkie White, was a veteran slugger. He was supposed to be a big step up in class. Chalkie had once held the number 9 spot in the top 10. But White's best days were behind him now. He traded freely with Jackson in the first round. He gave ground in the second. In the fourth round, White sat down under a series of hard punches. Jackie was sure that he would get up before the 10 count, but Chalkie just sat there. He had had enough.

After the Chalkie White fight, Jackson started baking bread. He was getting better at reading the cookbooks. After the breads, he started trying cakes and, finally, pies. He trained as hard as ever, but much of the time now he wondering how to make a perfect crust. Pie after pie came out of Madeline's oven. None of them had quite the perfect crust, however.

In his 11th bout, Jackie fought Ruben Gonzales from Los Angeles. The fight was a tough one. Before Jackie hammered out Gonzales in the eighth, the Mexican fighter rebroke Jackie's nose.

Chapter 8

The night that Jackson won his 11th fight was the 11th of May. Madeline threw a surprise birthday party for him. There was a little cake with lots of candles. Jackie blew out the candles while everyone sang "Happy Birthday." He didn't bother to count the candles. And not wanting to spoil the party, he didn't tell anyone that it wasn't really his birthday.

"It was awful nice," he told Madeline later. "But today's not really my birthday. I told you that I don't have one, didn't I?"

Madeline laughed and smiled. "Sure, you told me that, Jackie. But it isn't right, not having a birthday. Everyone has a birthday. So I got to thinking. I looked in my diary, and sure enough, the day was just right. It was on May eleventh that I met you last year. And then May is your month, anyhow. Besides, tonight was your eleventh fight, and I just knew you'd win. And so, well, I said to myself, that's the day! My diary doesn't lie, Jackie.

"I've already put it down on the calendar. As far as I'm concerned, that's the day it's going to be! I figured, knowing you, that you'd be a decent sport about it. Right?"

"OK," said Jackie. "All right! Then today's my birthday."

"That's right, baby," said Madeline. "And here, here's a little something I got for you." She handed him a tiny package wrapped in colored paper and tied with a ribbon.

"What's this, Madeline?"

"It's a present. What's it look like? It's a birthday present."

"Oh," said Jackie. Slowly, he opened his birthday present. It was the first birthday present he'd ever had. Inside the tiny package was a small gold locket. It was shaped like a heart. With the locket was a heavy gold neck chain. Inside the locket was a little photo of Madeline.

"I hope you like it, baby," she said.

"Like it?" asked Jackie. "Like it? Shoot, I love it!"

When she put it around his neck, he felt tears running down his cheeks. He tried to stop them, but they kept flowing, unchecked, warm and wet on his face. "Look at me," sobbed Jackie, "crying like a baby."

"You go on and cry," said Madeline. She held him close in her strong arms. "You go right on and cry all you like. You got a right to."

The next night, Jackie baked what Madeline swore was the perfect pie crust.

The week after that, Frankie Carbella told him that they were going to head for Los Angeles. It was the home of the real matchmaking. L.A. was the center of the ring action. Los Angeles, said Frankie, was the land of the big money fights.

Chapter 9

On the plane ride west, Jackie thought about what he would like to do. He'd have a few more fights, put away some good money, and then quit the business. He and Madeline could get married, if she'd have him.

When he was with Madeline, he had started reading. At first, he had just looked at cookbooks and magazines. Then he started reading the newspaper. Madeline had helped him. She had worked with him, and he had improved. He'd improved quite a lot, in fact. He was even starting to read books now. Real books, big ones, even. He read stories about faraway places with people who did different things.

Madeline had even showed him how to work some math problems. Frankie had given him a written contract. From now on, Frankie would get 40 percent of the purse. Jackie asked around at the gym about this. The other fighters said it was a fair deal. Some of the managers took 50 percent or more. Madeline showed Jackie how to figure out his share. If the purse was for $1,000, then Frankie would get $400. Jackie would get $600.

On the plane ride west, he thought about other things—about things he had read. Somewhere, he had read that the human brain had two sides. One side of the brain was supposed to be in charge of figuring things out. The other side of the brain was for feelings. It told you how you felt, who you loved, all kinds of things like that.

And he had a brain, too! He was more than sure of it now. OK, it was true—he was built just right for a middleweight fighter. He had those lean, hard legs. They were long, skinny legs that made him taller than most of the guys he fought. And his upper body was big. His shoulders and chest were big and solid from years of running turkey guts. And he did have a big punch. He could knock people out with either hand. The managers said he had heart— whatever that was.

But he was getting hit in every fight. Getting hit hard, too. His head was getting jarred, smashed, and slammed. In his sparring sessions now, he could almost feel those little gray brain cells dying. He could feel it every time he took a hard hit to the head.

And the guys he was fighting were just stiffs like him, trying to make a living. It didn't seem right, beating their heads in like he did. Maybe he was getting soft. Maybe he was thinking too much now. He wasn't sure.

Chapter 10

"In this corner! At one hundred and fifty-nine pounds. With a record of eleven wins and no losses. With eleven knockouts!" yelled Jimmy Lennon, the ring announcer. "The pride of St. Paul, Minnesota—Jackson Oaks Fernandez!" And Jackie was off and fighting in Los Angeles.

In the next two months, Frankie put him in four fights that would be fairly easy. Jackson won all of them by knockouts. His name was now a drawing card. His record was perfect: all wins, all knockouts. He called Madeline after each fight and gave her all the details. As to when he was coming home, he wasn't sure.

There was big money to be made in California. And there were also women in California—lots and lots of them. They were starting to notice him, too. Jackson's name and picture were in the sports pages all the time now.

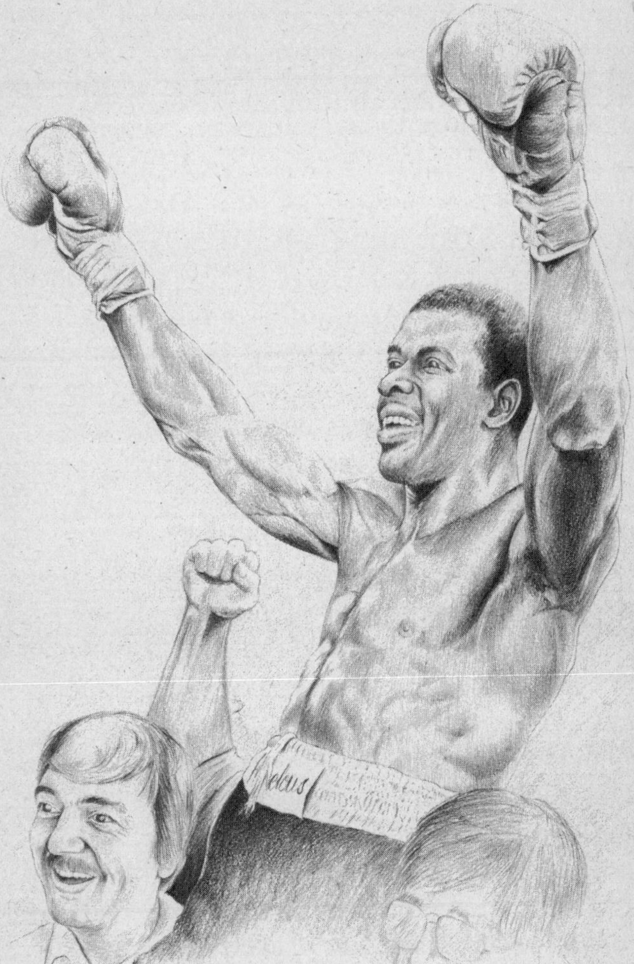

In Stockton, California, he fought Rocky L.L. Synder. The L.L. stood for "love 'em and leave 'em," they said. Snyder was a pretty good fighter. He was another step up in class. Snyder was ranked 10th in the world. If Jackie beat him, he was to get a bigger fight with Sailor Sands. In the sixth round of their fight, Jackie belted L.L. Snyder out.

He met Sailor Sands in Oakland. Sands was ranked seventh in the top 10. Jackie finished off the Sailor at the start of the ninth round.

After the Sailor fight, Jackie's popularity soared. There was a big write-up on him in *Ring* magazine. He was picked as their Fighter of the Month. *Ring* magazine now had Jackie ranked as the sixth best 160-pound fighter in the world.

Frankie Carbella was also riding high these days. With almost every fight, the money got better. Besides Jackson, Frankie also had a heavyweight fighter. The heavyweight was also unbeaten. Carbella bought himself a new Cadillac. He asked Jackie if he didn't need one, too. Jackie declined, though. He still liked to stash away most of his money in the bank.

Six weeks after the Sailor fight, Jackie fought Ernesto Rocos. Rocos was a good young middleweight from Los Angeles. Like Jackie, he had lost no fights. Rocos was said to be a very "hungry" fighter. Halfway through the first round, Rocos caught him with a solid left hook to the temple. The punch dropped Jackie to the canvas. Jackie got up and kept fighting. He fought this fight as though in a deep, foggy dream. Somewhere in one of the late rounds of the battle, the referee held Jackie's hand up high.

Jackie sensed more than actually heard the roaring of the crowd. It was almost a week before he felt halfway normal again. The fight with Rocos was called the Fight of the Year by the *Los Angeles Times*. Jackie's victory over Rocos earned him almost $5,000. He also got a badly rebroken nose and 13 stitches over the eyes.

The Rocos fight also made Jackie the new star of the L.A. fight crowd. Suddenly, he was invited everywhere. Women—black women, white women, Latin and Oriental women—took notice of him. They whispered sweet things in his ear. They fought over him at parties in Beverly Hills. And Jackie resisted none of it.

Before all this, he had never drunk or smoked. At most, he had had just a few beers now and then. But now, he was drinking champagne. He was smoking Cuban cigars. He was swimming in beautiful women.

After the Rocos fight, he forgot to call Madeline. It was days later when he remembered, and then he let it pass. A month later, he was matched with a local tough guy from Sacramento. He knocked out this man without even working up a sweat.

One afternoon, Jackie was sitting in a lounge chair near the pool of some friend of Frankie's. He suddenly thought of Minnesota. It was a fine, warm day in Los Angeles. In Minnesota, it would be cold now. There would be ice and plenty of snow. Why anyone would want to live back there was hard to imagine. Out here in California, they had everything. There was sunshine and money. And more women than a guy could count. The people were nice, too. Everyone seemed so friendly out here in golden California.

Frankie Carbella often talked about going back to the Twin Cities. There always seemed to be some big fight out west to take care of first, though.

Jackson trained less hard now than before. Some mornings now, he would sleep in rather than get up and do his roadwork. But Frankie watched over his prize middleweight plum with care. He set up a series of matches with bums and has-beens. None of them were really all that good. Jackson punched them out, one after the other.

On May 11th, Jackson knocked out Johnny Burns in San Diego. After the party that followed the fight, Jackson lay awake in bed.

It was his birthday tonight, but no one knew it. No one knew it except Madeline. Maybe she didn't even know it any longer. He hadn't called her in months now. By now, she could be married to some doctor. Who knew?

He thought of the girls he had met in California. They were pretty girls, all of them. But they didn't really care about him. They just wanted to go out with a fighter, a tough guy, a future champion of the world.

Before he fell asleep, Jackie played with the golden locket that he still wore around his neck. He hardly ever opened the locket anymore. It was now mostly just a good-luck piece.

Chapter 11

Early in July, they took a trip to Seattle, where Jackson punched out Sammy Domingo in three rounds. In August, he fought Ricky "Bossman" Caldwell back in Los Angeles and cooled him in the fourth.

Frankie was now trying to set up a title fight with the Champ. He constantly nagged Jackie to train harder, to run farther.

In October, Jackie fought Bill Scott of London, England. Scott was ranked the number one contender in the world. For the first time in more than a year, Jackie was the underdog.

Scott ran from him in the first round. He kept Jackie off balance in the second. Scott beat him to the punch in the third, fourth, and fifth rounds. In the sixth round, he tried to punch Jackie out.

Jackie reeled from the punches. His left eyebrow was split open. His nose was pulverized. His mouth felt like hot mush. Scott poured it on, flooding him with blows, some soft, some hard, some harder. Jackson, true to form, took the punches and slugged back. In the next round, the seventh, he thought he felt the Englishman weaken slightly. Whenever Jackie hit him with a solid shot to the body, he heard the man grunt.

Now it was Jackson's turn to pour it on. He smashed Scott with hard shots to the ribs. He uppercut and rabbit-punched him in the clinches. The Englishman butted him in a clinch. Jackson hit him low and was warned by the referee.

In the next clinch, Scott thumbed him in the eye. Jackson threw the man away from him, up against the ropes, and started slamming him. The London fighter sagged. The referee just watched. Jackson hit some more. He crunched the man with everything he had. The man's head bounced back and forth like the speedbag in the gym. Suddenly, Jackson thought he heard something. He stepped back, unsure, and Scott fell face forward to the canvas.

The crowd roared. Jackson looked down at the fallen fighter. The man tried to gain his feet, but fell back to his knees. The Englishman's eyes were nothing more than slits in a pulp of a face. His nose looked almost square. Blood covered the man, some of it his, much of it Jackson's.

Now Jackson Fernandez himself was the number one contender for the middleweight title.

Jackie no longer went to late parties or slept late in the mornings. Once again, he ran his seven miles every morning. At night, he now went to bed early in the evening. In the gym, he beat the heavy bags until his hands ached. At night, he soaked them in warm water and Epsom salts.

He wasn't sure why, but he started reading books again. He also started cooking meals for himself. He ate alone in his room.

A title fight with the Champ was now set for February 2nd, Groundhog Day. They were to fight in Las Vegas, Nevada. Win or lose, Jackson's purse was to be $75,000. He worked out his cut on paper the way Madeline had showed him. Frankie would get $30,000 for the fight. Jackie would get $45,000.

Christmas came 'round. Jackson turned down all invitations to go out and party. He spent Christmas Day alone in his room.

On New Year's Eve, he broke training and went to a big bash in the Hollywood Hills. He had too much to drink and danced with a genuine movie star. The rest of the month, he trained. On February 2nd, he stepped into the ring with the Champ.

Chapter 12

For a month now at least, everyone had been giving him advice on how to handle the Champ. The guy had it all, they said. The Champ wasn't like other fighters. He could outpoint you with his fancy moves and fast hands. He could stiff you with either left or right. The Champ had been fighting for almost 10 years. He hadn't lost a fight in almost eight years straight. Almost everyone who fought him was knocked out.

But the Champ had been at it a long time. His time had come. He was ripe for the picking. He was probably over the hill, but you had to be careful. The Champ was tricky. He fooled people.

As the referee gave them the rules, Jackson looked at the man who was the middleweight champion of the world. Often, as the rules were being given, his opponents had glared at him.

They tried to put a scare into him. Some of his other opponents would just stare at the floor. They took no chance of being scared themselves. This man, though, just smiled. He was a handsome man, the Champ. There was nothing scared or angry about this man at all. The Champ looked like a rich kid on Christmas morning. This guy enjoyed fighting. It was his purest element.

* * *

Jackson started the fight slowly, circling and jabbing, moving to his own left. The Champ was far from slow, but Jackson was able to reach him often with his jab. In the second round, he jabbed and left it out a trifle too long. The Champ punched over his jab and caught him flush with an overhand right. The punch, however, didn't feel all that solid to Jackson. He counter-punched and won the round on all the cards.

The third and fourth rounds were almost exact repeats of the second. The Champ kept finding the range with the overhand right. Jackson kept answering him with stiff countering shots. In his corner, the handlers warned him to stay cool, not to underestimate this man. In the fifth round, Jackson connected with three solid blows and sensed the man slowing down.

In the sixth round, the Champ again caught him flush with the right hand over his jab. But there seemed to be nothing much on the man's punch. Jackson grew in confidence. He danced around the ring. He dusted the champion of the world with lefts and rights. With 20 seconds left in the round, he backed the Champ into a corner. He stuck him with the jab and saw the Champ's overhand right coming in return. Ignoring the blow, Jackson cut loose with his own right hand, but this time the champion's right hand exploded across his face.

"Four, five!" he heard the referee counting. "Six! Seven! Eight!" and Jackson climbed to his feet.

The referee shook his gloves clean and looked into his eyes. "You all right?" he asked.

"Sure," said Jackson. His knees felt like Jell-O.

From the neutral corner, the Champ swooped down on him. Across the man's face was a wide and handsome smile. The Champ grunted loudly and threw a roundhouse left. Jackson raised his gloves to block the blow. It never came. Instead, the Champ slammed him with another right. Jackson didn't see the punch coming. He didn't notice the next left hook that took him flush on the ear. Nor did he ever see the last overhand right that dropped him, legs twitching, floundering on the canvas under the bright Las Vegas lights.

In his corner, they stuck smelling salts under his swollen nose. "Did I beat him?" he asked his cornermen.

"No, man," they said. "He sucker-punched you. You was punched out."

As he walked away toward the dressing room, no one slapped him on the back. Many fans had bet good money on him and had lost. They booed as he passed. Just as he was leaving the arena, someone in the crowd doused him from behind with a cup of warm beer.

Chapter 13

Back in Los Angeles, Jackie slept late in the mornings. No longer did he feel the urge to get up and go running. Frankie Carbella told him that it could have happened to anyone. He wasn't done yet. There would be plenty more fights. Lots more paydays. Maybe even another chance at the Champ in a year or so.

For a week, Jackie stayed holed up in his room. When he wanted something, he called for room service. On the 10th day of the month, he left the hotel, taking a cab to the airport. He thought about telling Frankie that he was leaving but decided to hell with it. He owed the man nothing. Frankie had done all right by him.

At the airport, Jackie took the first flight he could get to St. Paul. The ride back took less than three hours. It was 16 degrees below zero when he arrived. As he stepped from the plane, the cold air gripped him. He suddenly felt alive again.

He started to walk from the airport. After two blocks in his thin California clothes, he got smart and stopped a cab. Where he wanted to go was to Madeline's place, but as he neared her block, he lost heart. He had the cab driver drop him off at a motel just a few blocks away.

In the room, he unpacked his suitcase and climbed into the cold bed. As he lay there, he felt as if his arms and legs were miles long. As though his head were far, far away from his feet. It seemed as if there really was no one named Jackson Oaks Fernandez. It was just a made-up name anyhow, wasn't it?

The ceiling of the room looked as if it were a football field away. He thought of Frankie Carbella. What would the guy say when he found that Jackie was gone? Probably Frankie would try to find him. Jackson Fernandez, the fighter, was still good for more money. For bigger purses.

No one else would be looking for him. Certainly, none of those women from Los Angeles would be. The fancy women didn't care much for losers. But he didn't give a hoot. Not him.

He didn't give a damn.

It didn't bother him. He was tough, hard. Nothing bothered him.

It was 5:30 in the morning before he fell asleep at last.

All through the next day he slept. When he awoke, he took a shower, went out, and ate at a cafe near the motel. Afterwards, he walked down the street and entered the first bar he came to. It was dark in the bar. He sat alone in a corner and drank brandy-and-sodas. He had learned about the drink in Los Angeles.

After six or seven brandies, he got up and left the bar. He walked back to the motel and let himself into the dark and quiet room.

He sat on the double bed. The walls of the room seemed to close in on him. The ceiling seemed much lower than it had the night before. The whole room started to turn and then spin. He got up, went into the bathroom, and threw up his dinner and drinks in the toilet.

Back on the bed, he closed his eyes and tried to sleep. But sleep was a poor joke. Again he felt himself growing distant from his body. He looked at his feet, and again they looked miles away. There were people in this motel. Lots of other people locked away in their rooms. But they didn't know he was here in this room, so close to them. They didn't know, didn't care. He was alone. But then, he'd always been alone, actually. Ever since he was a tiny baby.

He raised his hand. It looked far away from him, too. He raised the hand to his face to wipe away his tears. But his face was dry. Even his tears ignored him now. He ran the hand down over his face. He felt the scar tissue over his eyes from the hundreds of blows. He felt his mashed-up nose. Across his face ran the hand, and then it stopped at his neck. He felt the cool hardness of the heavy gold chain. Ah, he thought, that chain! Something real! He sat up in the bed and opened his eyes. He pulled the locket open and looked at the photo. From within the tiny golden heart, Madeline smiled at him.

Jackson jumped up from the bed. He looked at the clock. It was just after two in the morning. Dressing quickly, he threw on his jacket and bolted from the little room.

It was snowing outside. He jogged, slowly at first and then faster, toward Madeline's apartment. Many things raced through his mind as he ran. Perhaps she wasn't home. Maybe she had moved and wasn't even there. But it was possible that she was home. It was also possible that she was there and had some man with her. Well, tough! He'd punch the sucker out! No, no, he wasn't going to do that at all. He would just say that he was sorry. That was all. He'd say he was sorry and leave.

Rounding the corner, he ran up to her place. As he walked the stairs to her door, he felt himself growing gutless, but went ahead, anyway. At her door, he started to knock, then held himself back. Who in the hell was he to be banging at her door at this time of night? It was such a long time now since he'd left. All that time, and he hadn't even bothered to call or write. He hadn't sent her a present on her birthday. Nothing. Maybe she wouldn't even remember who he was.

"Oh, go on!" he told himself. "Go on. Knock on the door. Now!" And at last he did, softly at first, then harder.

"Who's there?" asked a woman's voice. "Who is it?"

It sure sounded like her. "It's me," he said. His voice sounded small and weak to him.

"Who is it?" she asked again.

"It's me, Madeline," he said louder. "It's me, Jackie Fernandez."

The closed door swung open, and there was Madeline. Her hair was mussed with sleep. She wore an old, faded, flannel nightgown. She looked perfectly beautiful to him. "Jackie!" she screamed. "Is it really you?"

"Yep," he said, "I guess it is." Madeline pulled him inside, threw her arms around him, and held him close. For minutes, they held each other, saying nothing.

"So," said Madeline at last. "All this time. All this time, and not a word. Nothing. I should throw you out, shouldn't I?"

61

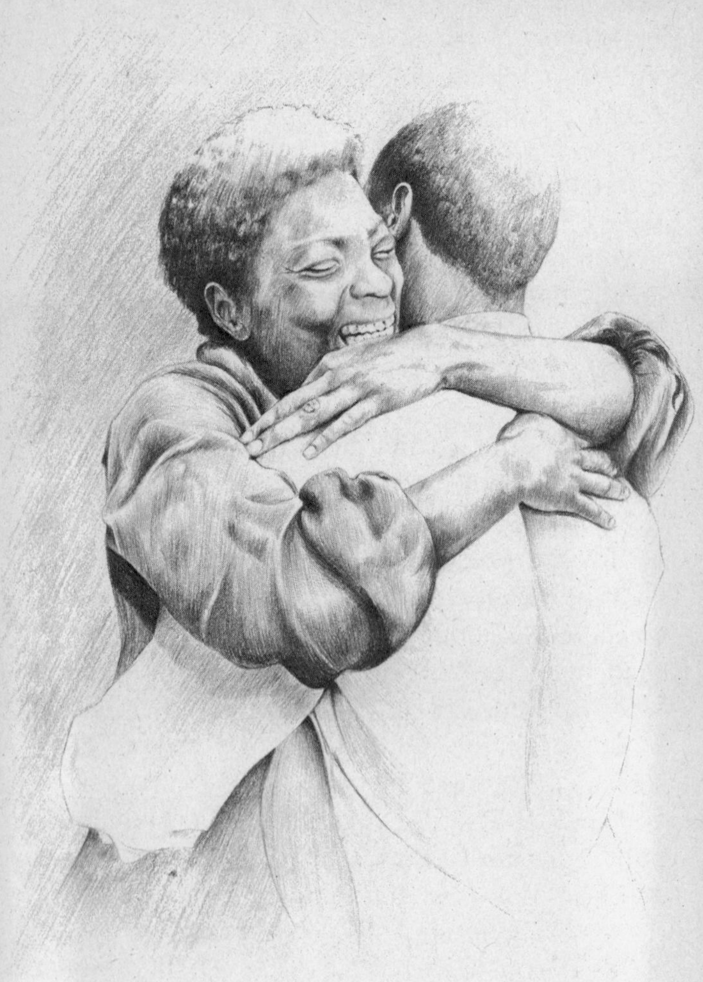

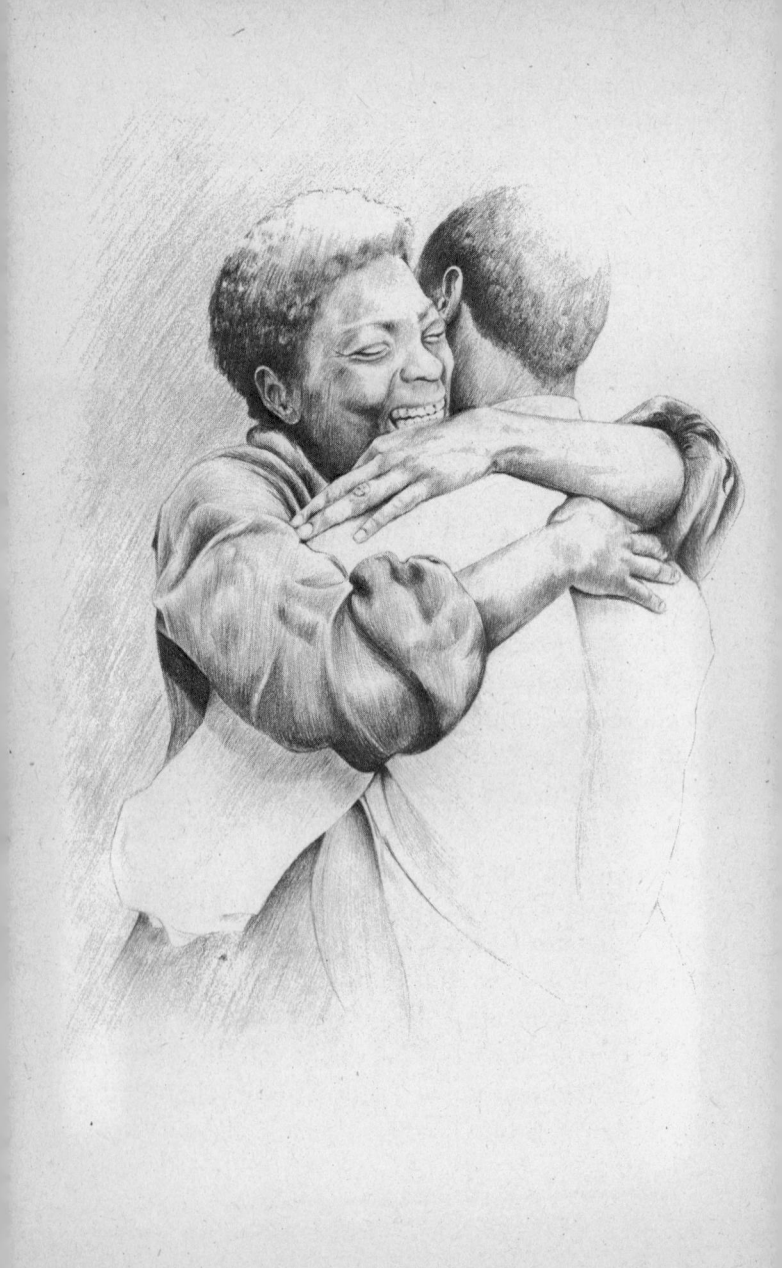

Jackson said nothing. She was right. She ought to toss him out.

"But I couldn't do that," she said. "And I wouldn't really want to. I heard you didn't win the title. I'm awfully sorry about that."

"I'm not," he said. "It doesn't matter. I'm just, well—" And then he couldn't talk anymore. Big tears ran freely down his cheeks, real tears this time, wet and salty.

"Don't talk, baby," said Madeline. "We can talk about it later."

Epilogue

Three months later, spring was in the air. The days were getting longer. The nights were growing warmer. The poplar trees along the Mississippi River were leafing out again. The wild ducks were once more returning to Minnesota. The snow and ice had all gone for the season. And with the coming of spring, Jackson started the restaurant.

It wasn't much of a restaurant, really, more of a cafe. But Jackson did all of the cooking. The hamburgers were pretty good there, said people who knew. And the pies—ah, the pies were great! The pie crusts were almost perfect.

Madeline kept her job at the hospital after they got married. She enjoyed being a nurse. And the restaurant was his baby, after all. But it was Madeline who thought of the name. "Let's name it after you, Jackie," she said.

And so came to be that little cafe, The Birthday Boy's Place.